Unearthing Garden

mysteries

EXPERIMENTS FOR KIDS

Ellen Talmage

Photographs by Bruce Curtis

fulcrum kids
Golden, Colorado

i

Library of Congress Cataloging-in-Publication Data
Talmage, Ellen.
  Unearthing garden mysteries : experiments for kids / Ellen Talmage; photographs by Bruce Curtis.
    p. cm.
Includes bibliographical references (p.   ) and index.
  ISBN 1-55591-993-6 (pbk. : alk. paper)
  1. Gardening—Juvenile literature. 2. Botany—Experiments—Juvenile literature. 3. Garden ecology—Experiments—Juvenile literature. [1. Plants—Experiments. 2. Botany—Experiments. 3. Garden ecology—Experiments. 4. Ecology—Experiments. 5. Experiments.]
I. Curtis, Bruce, ill. II. Title.
  SB457 .T25 2000
  580'.78—dc21
00-010012

Book design: Ann W. Douden

Printed in China
0 9 8 7 6 5 4 3 2 1

Fulcrum Publishing
16100 Table Mountain Parkway, Suite 300
Golden, Colorado 80403
(800) 992-2908 • (303) 277-1623
www.fulcrum-resources.com

this book is dedicated to cousins everywhere!

contents

acknowledgments

This book could not have been written without the help of many people. To the students from Rooms 10 and 12 at Riley Avenue School in Calverton, New York, and their teachers, Catherine Kent and Shirley Romer: Thanks for testing so many of the experiments for me. And to Dan Gilrein, Cornell University Entomologist (or as school kids call him, "Dan, Dan the Bug Man"): Your advice, photographs, and enthusiasm for this book were invaluable; I couldn't have done it without you.

Thanks also to Peggy Webb of Beckett Lake Garden Center in Clearwater, Florida, for allowing some young scientists to use your facility. To my dear friends Lela Kelly and Suzanne Bennett, and my cousins the Brickley family, for arranging my work excursions with Bruce to Florida. To Marc Benedict, for designing a workable "worm condo" on AutoCad. To my mom, Carol, and sister, Laurie, for helping me coordinate things on the home front. And last but not least, thanks to my husband, Terry, and my son, Cory, for putting up with me during the writing process.

PHOTO BY ELLEN TALMAGE

foreword

PHOTO BY
DAN
GILREIN

Hello! My name is Ellen Talmage, but my friends call me the Horticultural Goddess. My mission in this book is not only to entertain you, but also to enlighten you about one of Mother Nature's most important domains—the world of plants.

The projects featured here are simple, and the materials are easy to find. If your results differ slightly, don't get frustrated. Remember that the intent of each project is to have fun, while also learning a little something in the process. And if you have a flop or two, don't get discouraged. It happens to every scientist. Remember that short-term failure brings long-term success. Together we'll figure out how to transform that backyard garden and houseplant jungle of yours into a laboratory of endless wonder and fun.

Hold on to your garden hat and get out your journal, pencil, and magnifying glass: Here we go!

introduction

Because plants are such an intrinsic part of everyday life, we can tend to overlook and even become disenchanted with them. Kids are no exception. Ask them if they think plants are exciting and they'll likely tell you "no." Although many kids understand that we could not live on Earth without plants as a source for food, shelter, and oxygen, how many really appreciate the diversity and splendor of the plant kingdom? Read on to discover 20 projects guaranteed to excite kids about the fascinating world of plants.

Many of these projects were designed with the National Science Education Standards in mind, making this book a perfect resource for use in the classroom as well as at home. Many of the required materials will be readily available in most classrooms and homes; everything else can be obtained through Carolina Biological Supply Company, P.O. Box 6010, Burlington, NC 27216-6010, (800) 334-5551, or through your local garden center.

Unearthing Garden Mysteries is organized into four sections. The first, "Plant Experiments," presents a variety of simple projects using inexpensive, easy-to-find materials. The next section, "Exploring the World," is dedicated to helping kids learn firsthand just how adaptable plant life can be. The third section, "Projects for Fun," is meant to get kids out of their chairs and into some hands-on fun. Last but not least is the "Critters" section, a collection of projects featuring the small creatures that live among plants in cooperative (and sometimes not so cooperative) relationships.

Plan to work side by side with kids, showing them how to do things safely. Note that the project "Building a Worm Condo" involves some use of power tools—a job strictly for adults—in preparing the condo materials for assembly, although kids can of course take an active role during the actual assembly process. Adults should also be present to monitor the use of fertilizers and any other potentially harmful materials and tools.

Plant Experiments

don't be so sensitive!

INTRODUCTION

Have you ever heard the saying "Don't be so sensitive"? It is often used after someone reacts defensively to being criticized. Plants aren't people, of course, but let's take a closer look at a particular plant: *Mimosa pudica*, also known as "sensitive plant." It can react in a way that seems almost human.

materials

Jiffy Pots or a cardboard or Styrofoam egg carton
Mimosa pudica seeds
Potting soil
4-inch pots
Fertilizer
Magnifying glass
Wristwatch
Journal and pencil

what to do

1. Sprinkle seeds onto the surface of moistened Jiffy Pots or onto the surface of a cardboard or Styrofoam egg carton filled with moistened potting soil.
2. Cover the seeds with a thin layer of potting soil and place the Jiffy Pots or egg carton in a sunny windowsill.

Sprinkled seeds on moist soil.

After germination, be sure to keep the seedlings evenly moist.

3. After six weeks, transplant the plants to the larger containers. Keep one plant for yourself, and give the extras to friends and family (especially to those who are overly sensitive).

4. Fertilize your plant every three to four weeks, following instructions on the fertilizer package.

5. Observe the position of the plant's leaves during the day and again at night. Sketch each position in your journal.

6. During the day, brush your hand across the top of the plant several times and watch what happens.

7. Using the wristwatch, time the number of seconds it takes for the leaves to collapse. Record the number in your journal.

8. Time the number of minutes it takes for the plant to recover to its normal day position. Record the number in your journal.

9. Repeat steps 5–8 two more times.

10. Calculate the average collapse time by adding together the individual collapse-time measurements and dividing by 3.

11. Calculate the average recovery time by adding together the individual recovery-time measurements and dividing by 3.

Observe plant at night.

PHOTO BY DAN GILREIN

Touch plant.

- What other plants from the projects in this book have a similar response to day and night?
- Using a magnifying glass, examine the stem of the plant. What is growing out of the stem? Draw a picture of the stem. Why do you think the stem has developed this feature?
- Describe in your journal what happened to the leaves of the plant after being touched. How long did they stay like that?
- What is the purpose of calculating the average collapse and recovery times?

Sensitive plants before being touched.

Wilted leaves seconds after being touched.

explanation

The daytime and nighttime positions of *Mimosa pudica*, as with many plants, can be explained through circadian movements. The plant's daytime and nighttime positions differ from each other because the leaves of this plant have two different positions based on a predictable biological cycle in a 24-hour period. During the daylight hours the leaves are held out straight so they can capture the sunlight needed for the plant to make its food. At night when the "kitchen is closed" the leaves collapse so that they may sleep.

After touching this plant several times during the day, it is easy to understand why *Mimosa pudica* has the common name "sensitive plant." When touched, its leaves quickly droop down as if by magic. A few seconds later, the petioles drop and the pinnules fold together. This so-called magic can be explained through science. Through the sensory cells on its petioles, the plant converts your touch into an electric charge. This electric charge moves quickly down through the stem by way of specialized motor cells, which shrink when they receive the charge. As these cells shrink, the petioles drop. After a while, the cells begin to refill with fluid, which causes the leaves to return to their normal position.

Because no two plants will react to touch in exactly the same way, it is a good idea to calculate average times for collapse and recovery, so you can better understand your data. If you know the average collapse and recovery times, it is easier to predict what will happen the next time you touch the plant. Scientists use averaging a lot in their research; it is a very important mathematical tool.

Watch the stems collapse.

conclusion

A "sensitive plant" is actually more shocking (electrically speaking) than sensitive.

say your prayers and go to sleep

INTRODUCTION

Some plants look different at night than they do during the day. Let's take a closer look at two plants that "sleep" at night. Just as some people like to sleep on their stomachs, while others like to sleep on their backs, clover and prayer plants take their favorite positions as they catch some zees.

materials

Prayer plant (4-inch pot or larger)
Clover plant or clover seed
4-inch pot
Potting soil
Medium-sized cardboard box
Can of black spray paint
Magnifying glass
Journal and pencil

what to do

1. Clover plants (*Trifolium pratense*) are very common. From late spring through early fall, you can probably find them growing just outside your

Spray paint box for experiment.

door in a grassy area. If so, dig one up and plant it in a small pot. If not, order seed and grow your own clover. (Plant the seed according to the instructions on its package; it will take about six weeks to grow a good-sized clover plant.)

2. Borrow or purchase a prayer plant (*Maranta leuconevra*) and place it beside the clover plant. In your journal, record the movements of the leaves for both plants by sketching them in the early morning, in the late afternoon, and in the evening before you go to bed.

3. Spray paint the cardboard box black, inside and out (be sure to do this outdoors, because spray-paint fumes are harmful if inhaled; the paint will dry faster, too). Apply a second and a third coat if needed.

4. Place the black box over the plants during daylight hours. After one hour, remove the box and sketch the leaf positions of both plants. Replace the box over the plants and repeat your sketching after two hours, and then again after four hours. (It is important to note the time that you first place the box over the plants, so you will know when to remove it and make your sketches.)

5. Repeat step 4 another day, but this time put the plants in a dark closet instead of using the black box to remove their natural light source.

observations

- Based on your evening observations, which of the two plants gets into its nighttime position faster? Take a closer look at the leaves themselves.

Nighttime position of leaves.

Rainy-day position (low light) of leaves.

Sunny-day position of leaves.

Do the leaves of both the prayer plant and the clover plant move in the same direction (up and down) during the night? In your journal, describe how the leaf movement is different for each plant.

- Based on your daytime observations (using the black box and the dark closet), do both plants actually get into their nighttime positions when their natural light source is removed? If so, how long did it take? Take a closer look at the leaves themselves. Do the leaves of both the prayer plant and the clover move in the same direction when their natural light source is removed? In your journal, describe how the leaf movement is different for each plant.

Observe the plant after lifting off the black box.

explanation

Because neither plant responded well to being put in the dark during daylight hours, you can conclude that there is something more to nighttime leaf movements than simply the absence or presence of light. By giving the plants two different darkened situations to close their leaves (in a box and in a closet), you can safely conclude that each plant had plenty of chances to do its thing.

The phenomenon of changing daytime and nighttime leaf positions is explained by circadian rhythms. Simply put, this means the plants' movements are governed by an internal clock that tells them when to open and close their leaves. Many forms of life have such an internal clock. Bears know when to hibernate and plants know when to say their prayers and go to sleep.

Using a magnifying glass, take a closer look at the two test plants. On the clover plant, examine the area where the three leaflets meet the stem. There are little, pimplelike swellings of the stem that are filled with water. When the bottoms of these pimples have no water in them, the leaflets drop into their nighttime position.

Each time the black box was removed during daylight hours, the results were the same—no nighttime position.

When the pimples are filled with water, the leaflets rise and open to receive the sunlight, so the plant can make its food for the day.

The prayer plant moves in a different way. Take a closer look at its stem, at the point where it meets the leaf. You will notice that there is a section about ¼ inch long that has a darker coloration. This special section holds different amounts of water at different times of the day. The swelling of this section causes the leaves to fold up, looking like hands praying. To demonstrate how this works, put your elbows on a table and bend back your wrists. Notice how your palms are facing upward? Your palm (like the blade of the leaf) is now exposed to light from above (sunlight). When nighttime comes, the stem of the prayer plant fills with water on both sides, so the leaf actually folds up.

Can you figure out how this plant got its name?

PHOTOS BY DAN GILREIN

conclusion

Both clover plants and prayer plants have different leaf positions at night compared to those during the day, and their different leaf movements are based on circadian rhythms rather than just the absence or presence of light.

Clover plants sleep with their leaves nodding down.

meet venus flytrap— if you dare!

INTRODUCTION

The Venus flytrap is a plant that in some ways acts more like an animal. Its scientific name is *Dionaea muscipula*, and it is a carnivorous plant that catches its food in a very dramatic way. It lures insects to visit its specially adapted leaf traps and then, as if possessing some sort of animal intelligence, captures them by folding up the tips of its traps. Let's see if we can explain this phenomenon.

The Venus flytrap comes from the damp, boggy areas of North and South Carolina. When the soil of this region was studied, it was found to contain very little nitrogen. Because all plants need nitrogen for healthy growth, the Venus flytrap had to adapt to stay in this environment. Other plants that didn't adapt disappeared, leaving the Venus flytrap with a home all to itself. How did the Venus flytrap adapt to get the precious nitrogen? It learned to trap insects and absorb the nitrogen from their decaying bodies.

Venus flytrap at work.

PHOTO BY DAN GILREIN

materials

- Venus flytrap
- Small bowl
- Magnifying glass
- Tweezers
- Tiny piece of chopped meat or a dead fly
- Journal and pencil

Watch what happens!

what to do

1. Remove the plastic packaging from the Venus flytrap (but don't remove the plant from its pot and soil).
2. Place the potted flytrap in a bowl.
3. Fill the bowl with an inch of room-temperature water.
4. Examine the plant's leaf traps with a magnifying glass.
5. Place the tip of a pencil inside one of the plant's fully developed, open leaf traps, touching the trap's trigger hairs with the pencil. Watch what happens and record your observations in your journal.
6. Repeat step 5 for the same leaf trap after it reopens.
7. Using tweezers, place the chopped meat or dead fly inside another fully developed, open leaf trap.

observations

- What happened when you touched the trigger hairs with the pencil? How long did it take for the leaf trap to reopen?
- When you repeated the action of touching the trigger hairs, did you get different results?

> **NOTE:**
> THE VENUS FLYTRAP SHOULD NOT BE GATHERED FROM ITS NATURAL HABITAT. ORDER NURSERY-PROPAGATED PLANTS AND FOLLOW THE ACCOMPANYING DIRECTIONS CAREFULLY.

- What happened to the leaf trap that you fed the meat or fly to? Did it reopen? If so, how long did it take? If not, what do you think is happening inside the leaf trap?

explanation

If you examine the tips of the leaf traps, you will see outward hairs that look like eyelashes. On the outsides of these eyelashes are tiny glands, which release a special liquid that attracts the flies, ants, and other insects the plant needs for food.

These eyelashes are specially sized to help the plant decide what is worth keeping for a meal. Many insects are attracted to a leaf trap because of the scent coming from the glands. The little insects that happen to land on trigger hairs can crawl out between the eyelashes after the trap has closed. The larger, meal-sized insects cannot, so they become dinner.

How does this trapping process actually work? On the inner surface of every leaf trap are specialized trigger hairs. There are at least six of these trigger hairs in every trap. Scientists still aren't exactly sure what causes such a quick closing reaction, but they will figure it out someday. In the meantime, enjoy the magic of your Venus flytrap. When you trick the plant into closing one of its traps, you will notice that the trap does not stay closed for more than a few hours. If you actually feed the plant, a trap can take up to a week or more to reopen.

Once a leaf trap reopens, it can usually be triggered again after a few days' rest. But you may find that this is not always the case. You will notice that, every 10 days or so, a new leaf trap begins to emerge from the center of the plant and soon develops into a fully functional trap. Mother Nature makes sure there is always a fresh mouth to feed.

conclusion

Try catching insects and feeding them live into the open traps of your plant with tweezers. If you accidentally trigger a leaf trap with your finger, don't worry—Venus flytraps don't bite hard, and they don't chew. It can take up to a week to digest all the nutritious nitrogen juice from a bug breakfast.

troubleshooting

Following the instructions that come with a Venus flytrap is very important if you plan to keep the plant for an extended period of time. By following the growing instructions, you are mimicking the plant's natural habitat. Be sure to grow your plant in standing water, provide high humidity, and provide it with a bright, indirect source of light, such as that from an east- or west-facing window. Remember that your plant comes from a warm climate, so do not attempt to grow it outside. It will need plenty of warmth to do well. If you buy a Venus flytrap from a store, its potting soil should already have plenty of nitrogen in it, so don't add plant food.

Sometimes the end of a leaf trap will turn black and die while a meal is being digested. If this happens, and if it appears that the blackness is spreading down the stem, just snip off the decaying trap with scissors. This practice will stop the spread of any disease and keep the plant looking nice.

Feed with a small bit of meat.

PHOTO BY DAN GILREIN

which way will the vine twine?

INTRODUCTION

A vine is a special kind of plant. It has a flexible stem that it wraps around another plant or object to help support itself. Let's try to figure out if all vines wrap their stems in the same direction.

materials

**Hyacinth bean
   seeds**
Two plastic cups
Potting soil
Fertilizer
**Two garden stakes
   (12-inches or longer)**
Camera and film
Journal and pencil

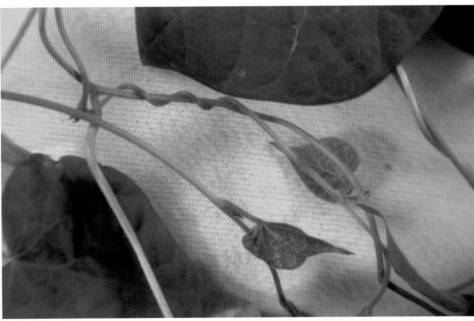

Vines love to twine.

PHOTO BY DAN GILREIN

what to do

1. Plant three bean seeds (according to the directions on the seed packet) in each of two plastic cups filled with moistened potting soil.

Plant the seeds.

2. Place the cups in a sunny windowsill and allow the plants to grow until the shoots are about 8 inches long. This will take six to eight weeks or less if you fertilize your bean cups.

3. Place a garden stake in the center of each cup. Wrap one set of vines clockwise around its stake (looking down over the top of the stake), and wrap the other set of vines counterclockwise.

4. After one week, take a picture for your journal showing the growth of the two plants. Take another picture after a second week of growth.

Label the markers as "clockwise" and "counter-clockwise."

observations

- Did you notice that one plant grew better than the other did? What do you think caused this?
- Go outdoors and explore the area for vines. Do they all wrap their stems in the same direction? Take pictures and add them to your journal.
- Why do you think vines have to wrap themselves around something?

explanation

The counterclockwise vines seem to grow better. Although both sets of vines do climb up their poles, the clockwise vines eventually rewrap themselves in a counterclockwise direction. A plant's tips are always attracted to sunlight so they follow the sun. A clockwise position also follows the sun, so this would be a logical conclusion.

Because vines have no means of support for themselves, they need to somehow find a way to get to the light of the sun. By climbing onto something else, they are able to grow upward, toward the sun, which increases their potential to survive.

Photograph the vines.

c o n c l u s i o n

Two plants of the same variety will naturally twine the same way.

t r o u b l e s h o o t i n g

When taking pictures outdoors, remember to keep your back to the sun (better yet, take pictures on a cloudy day). Indoors, remember to use a flash. Finally, whether outdoors or indoors, get close to your subject (but no closer than 3 feet) and remember to keep as still as possible when you snap your photos.

Photograph your subject with your back to the sun.

are daffodils shady ladies?

Shady Ladies.

PHOTO BY DAN GILREIN

INTRODUCTION

All plants have certain requirements to grow. Everyone knows that sunlight, water, and soil are all necessary for most plants to thrive. In this experiment, we'll be testing the sunlight requirement for daffodils.

We'll be working with two sets of plants of exactly the same type and exactly the same size, and we'll be growing them in the same soil and giving them the same amount of water. But we'll be varying the amount of sunlight they receive. In this way, by isolating the sunlight factor, we can measure whether the performance of their flowering is actually dependent on sunlight. Let's find out if shade makes a difference in the flowering performance of daffodils.

materials

12 daffodil bulbs
Bone meal fertilizer
Graph paper
Journal and pencil

what to do

1. In the fall, purchase 12 daffodils bulbs of exactly the same size and variety.
2. Select two sites in your yard where all conditions except sunlight are identical. One site should be on the east side of your house, close to the foundation, and the other site should be away from your house, fully exposed to sunlight.
3. For each site, dig 6 planting holes. Sprinkle bone meal fertilizer into the holes and plant your bulbs. (Follow the directions on the bulb packaging.)
4. In the early spring, start observing the daffodils' growth. Track results each week, for each test group, and chart your observations on a piece of graph paper. Keep track of which group flowers the most (this can be measured by tracking how long a single flower from the group stays in bloom), and which group produces the "showiest" flowering (this can be measured by tracking which group has the most flowers in bloom at any one time).
5. Repeat the observation process the next spring and then compare the results from the past two years. In your journal, record any differences between the two test groups.

observations

- Which group came up faster, the one out in the open or the one near the house?
- Which group flowered the longest?
- Which group produced the showiest flowering?
- Did results remain the same over both years?

Put some by the east side of the house.

PHOTO BY ELLEN TALMAGE

Record results clearly.

PHOTO BY ELLEN TALMAGE

explanation

The results of an experiment like this can vary greatly. Remember that although many factors are the same, some variation will occur in the amount of wind and rain a grouping of bulbs receives because of the orientation of weather patterns. If a storm is blowing from the east, the test group near the house will receive the wind and rain. If a storm comes from the west, the group on the east will be shielded from the wind and rain.

In the first year, all the bulbs should bloom nicely, a result of selecting bulbs all the same size. Generally, the bigger the bulb, the bigger the bloom. In fact, the size of the flower is predetermined by the bulb. In other words, the bulbs will bloom regardless of what you do to them.

The temperature of the soil heats up nicely next to a house foundation. This happens because of two things: Solar heat quickly warms the earth in a protected place, and waste heat radiates out of the basement. This extra heat allows the bulbs near the house to get a head start. The warmed bulbs near the foundation have a growing advantage every year in the early spring. But once the soil of the open ground area heats up, the exposed daffodils send out their leaves and flower buds in quick fashion and soon catch up to the daffodils protected by the house.

Observe the plants.

The biggest difference due to the varying light levels will show up the first year. Although all the plants should bloom the first year, the plants grown close to the house with a limited amount of sunlight will be taller and have weaker stems. After bulbs bloom, they need to make food for themselves for the next year's flowers. Because the house brings shade to the bulbs' leaves, they cannot make all the energy needed for producing strong flowers. Knowing this, do you think the bulbs near the house will be as showy in years to come?

conclusion

Generally, a bloom in the shade actually lasts longer than one in full sunlight, so you may find that an individual flower that lasts longer comes from next to the house. The showier grouping of plants will be the one in full sunlight. Generally, the sunnier the area, the showier the flowering.

As the years pass, you'll notice that the group exposed to light thrives, while the shaded group just survives and doesn't even flower after a while. The best thing to do is to dig up the hurting bulbs from the shade and move them into the sun. Within a year they will adjust to their new home and flower like crazy. Don't let that newly open spot of earth near your house discourage you. Get a shade-gardening book and find a plant that loves those conditions.

Enjoy the daffodils.

PHOTO BY
DAN GILREIN

a different kind of pumpkin patch

Choose a large pumpkin.

PHOTOS BY ELLEN TALMAGE

INTRODUCTION

Everyone knows that a pumpkin comes from a small seed, but how many people have actually grown their own pumpkins? If you have ever picked out your own pumpkin from the field, you have been in a pumpkin patch. Let's grow some pumpkin plants from seed and keep them on a sunny windowsill rather than in a pumpkin field. Instead of growing the pumpkin in a patch, we'll put a patch on the pumpkin plant. This patch will demonstrate how important sunlight is to plants.

Or choose a rotted pumpkin.

materials

- Large, mature pumpkin
- Large, sharp knife
- Newspaper
- Paper cups (the kind used for hot drinks)
- Potting soil
- Watering can
- Large plastic pot (10-inch or larger)
- Liquid fertilizer
- Black construction paper
- Scissors
- Paper clips
- Screwdriver
- Journal and pencil

what to do

1. Have an adult cut open a large, mature pumpkin (or you can wait until after Thanksgiving and use a rotting pumpkin).

2. Scoop out the seeds, spread them onto newspaper, and let them dry for a few days. In your journal, draw some life-sized pictures of the seeds, and record the date you collect them and how long it takes them to dry.

3. Fill several paper cups with potting soil.

4. Plant three pumpkin seeds in each cup, spacing seeds about one inch apart. Make sure that each seed is buried about one inch deep. Record in your journal the date that you plant the seeds.

5. Water the seed cups, so the moistened potting soil can settle around the seeds (making a dark moist place, which is favorable for seed germination).

6. Place the seed cups on a sunny windowsill.

7. When the roots on the pumpkin seedlings have reached the bottoms of the cups and the leaves are at least the size of apples, transplant the seedlings into a large pot. (Check the growth status by turning the cup over and gently lifting it off to observe the plant roots.)

8. Water the transplanted seedlings to force out any large air pockets in the soil. Fertilize the transplanted pumpkin plant every two weeks with a liquid fertilizer (follow instructions on the fertilizer package).

9. When one of the leaves is grapefruit-sized or larger, cut out two "patches" of exactly the same design from black construction paper (the patches should be smaller than the leaf). Paper clip one patch to the front side of the leaf, and paper clip the other to the back side of the leaf in exactly the same position.

10. Remove the patches periodically to examine the leaf for changes, making sure to reposition them in exactly the same position on the leaf each time you check it. Record your observations in your journal.

Have an adult cut open a fresh pumpkin.

Scoop out the seeds.

11. Once you have completed your observation of the patched leaf, remove the patches and allow the plant to grow freely in the windowsill (give it plenty of room to sprawl) until after the frost-free date.

12. When the weather is warm enough, transfer the pumpkin plant to a sunny spot in a garden.

13. When pumpkins begin to appear on the plant, select one or two to keep and pinch off the rest. This will cause the pumpkins you are growing to be as large as possible.

14. In August, when the pumpkins begin to mature, scratch designs or names into them using a screwdriver.

15. When your pumpkins have matured, select one, cut it open (with the help of an adult), and scoop out its seeds. In your journal, draw some life-sized pictures of these second-generation seeds.

Dry pumpkin seeds on a paper towel.

observations

- What did the original seeds feel like when they first came out of the pumpkin? How long did it take them to dry?
- How long did it take the planted seeds to germinate?
- What did the first leaves to emerge from the seeds look like? Did they look the same as the leaves that emerged later on? In your journal, draw pictures of the different types of leaves.
- How many days did it take for the patch pattern to appear on the leaf? In your journal, draw a picture of the pattern that developed. What happened after you removed the patches from the leaf?
- How does the pumpkin plant sprawl? Can you find the tiny, stringlike parts of the leaves called tendrils?
- What color are the flowers of the pumpkin plant? When did you first see them appear? Record this information in your journal.
- How do you think the flowers got pollinated? After you transferred the pumpkin plant outside, did you see any insects near the flowers, or do you think this job was accomplished by the wind?
- What did the developing pumpkins feel like when you wounded

Seed leaves are the first to emerge.

Time to transplant.

them with the screwdriver? What color is the scar tissue that developed over the wounded areas? Did your screwdriver designs grow evenly on the pumpkins? Record this information in your journal.

- In your journal, compare the pictures you drew of the original seeds to the pictures you drew of the second-generation seeds. Are the seeds the same size?

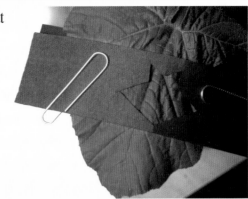

Place a patch on a leaf.

explanation

This project takes you through the entire life cycle of a pumpkin plant. Even if you only do parts of this project, you're sure to learn something.

The seeds that come out of the original pumpkin are quite moist, as the pumpkin itself is full of moisture. Setting the seeds out on an absorbent piece of paper keeps them from getting moldy. Clean, dry seeds seem to germinate best.

The first leaves to emerge from the seed are round and are called seed leaves, or cotyledons. The rest of the leaves take on the shape of regular pumpkin leaves. Seed leaves help a tiny plant switch over from being fed by the seed to feeding itself by making its own food later with its mature leaves.

When you attach patches to a leaf, the parts of the leaf that get no sunlight turn yellow. A plant leaf that gets no direct sunlight cannot complete the photosynthetic process. Without sunlight, the cells that contain chlorophyll cannot create sugars and oxygen from carbon dioxide and water. Because some of the cells in the leaf cannot perform the job they want to (because they aren't getting any sunlight), they turn yellow. The parts of the leaf that aren't covered by the patches remain green and happy because the cells in those parts are getting the sunlight they need. When you remove the patches, the leaf returns to its original color within a few

Remove the patch in two weeks.

The pumpkin's leaf turns fully green within a day of removing the patch.

days because the chlorophyll is always present in the leaf—it just can't be seen if it doesn't have the sunlight that it needs in order to turn green.

Scratching designs into the pumpkins is a fun part of this project. As the pumpkins continue to grow, the scratched areas become scarred with a tan-colored tissue. A pumpkin develops this scar tissue for the same reason that you as a human being develop a scab when you get a cut or a scratch. This natural defense mechanism keeps bad germs from entering the pumpkin. The design continues to grow with the pumpkin, but because the pumpkin's growth rate varies and depends on many factors (as with all growing things), the design usually grows unevenly.

When the time comes to cut open one of your pumpkins in late fall, you'll find that the second-generation seeds are exactly the same size as the original seeds. After drying them, you can store these seeds for up to one year if you keep them in a warm, dry place. If you are planting seed in a regular garden situation (a regular pumpkin patch), you should plant them very late in the spring.

conclusion

Pumpkins come in all shapes and sizes. The seed produced inside each pumpkin is preprogrammed to produce pumpkin offspring of much the same size, color, and texture. Seeds are pretty magical when you think about it—all that information packed into such a small package. With the proper conditions, a seed will produce a seedling, which in turn will grow into a full-sized pumpkin plant if given enough time, food, space, water, and sunlight. The leaves of a pumpkin plant are its food factory. Without sunlight, they cannot stay green—and cannot continue processing food for the plant.

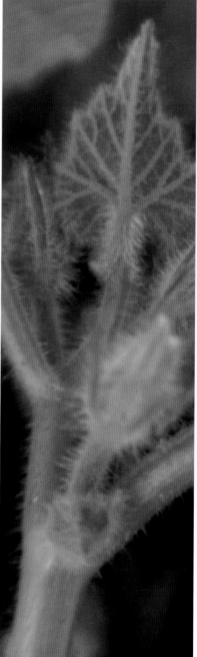

Pumpkin flower buds will eventually change into the orange fruit.

PHOTO BY DAN GILREIN

Exploring the World

there's fungus among us!

INTRODUCTION

A fungus is a very special kind of plant. The people who study fungi are called mycologists. Become a mycologist (even if just for a day) and explore the weird world that only the primitive, mysterious fungi can offer!

There are more than 250,000 kinds of fungi, making them the most numerous of all living creatures on Earth. All fungi are alike in that they do not have any green chlorophyll, which means that, unlike plants that make their own food, fungi must get their nourishment from other forms of life, whether it be plants or animals. Okay, all you mycologists out there, grab your journals. Let's explore!

Close-up of moldy bread.

PHOTO BY DAN GILREIN

materials

Cheese sandwich or slice of pizza
Collecting jar
Magnifying glass
Page from a self-sticking photo album
Cereal bowl
Journal and pencil

1. Number a page in your journal from 1 to 10.
2. Draw three columns down the right-hand side of the page, labeling them "Good," "Bad," and "Don't know."
3. Eat a cheese sandwich or slice of pizza for lunch.
4. Next to number 1 in your journal, write "Yeast." Yeast was used in making the food you just ate—it made the bread rise and helped process the cheese. Do you think yeast (a fungus) is good or bad for people? Check off the column that you think is the correct answer (if you don't know, check off the "Don't know" column).
5. Look in the refrigerator in the vegetable bin for some vegetables that may have gotten old. Can you find any mold? If so, you've found another fungus! Make an entry for "Mold" in your journal. Is it good or bad for people?
6. Let's keep going. Look in the bathroom in the shower. You probably won't be able to see anything, but know that this is a breeding area for a fungus that can cause athlete's foot, which makes the skin of a person's feet itch, crack, and burn. Keeping your shower clean helps prevent such fungus from growing there. Make an entry for "Athlete's foot" in your journal. Is it good or bad for people?
7. Ask your parents if you ever had ringworm as a young child. Ringworm is a fungal infection that causes round, scaly patches (usually about the size of a nickel) on a person's skin. It is contagious and needs to be treated with antifungal cream. Make an entry for "Ringworm" in your journal. Is it good or bad for people? (Don't start thinking all fungus except yeast is bad. Remember penicillin? This very important drug is produced from *Penicillium fungi.*)
8. Now it's time to hit the great outdoors. Not only do fungi feed off people (and animals), but they also feed off plants as well. Certain plants are the specific host plants for fungal rusts. See if you can find any of these (listed on the following page):

A mushroom (fungi) growing out of a bed of moss.

PHOTO BY DAN GILREIN

Barberry (shrub)
Cedar (tree)
Hollyhock (perennial)
Wheat (grass/grain)

If you can locate any of these plants, there is a good chance that you can find fungal rust on them. This disease looks just like the rust you might find on an old piece of metal. It tends to feed off very specific plants and can persist from year to year. Gather a couple of leaves that have rust on them and place them in your collecting jar. Try to infect another type of plant with the rust and you'll notice that the rust will not spread. This is because rust is very particular to its host plant and therefore causes no threat to plants on which it cannot feed. Make an entry for "Fungal rust" in your journal. If you were a wheat farmer, would you classify rust as being good or bad?

9. On to another fun fungus hunt—looking for the mushrooms. Go outdoors and start looking around in wooded areas that are full of dead or rotting trees (you can find mushrooms during the warmer part of spring, all through summer, and early into fall). Check observation sites often because many types of mushrooms appear and disappear almost overnight. You can also scout out mushrooms in shady spots on your lawn, and some types of mushrooms can even appear on the base of toilet bowls—so keep an eye out! Save some of your mushrooms for closer observation (see "Observations" below). Make an entry for "Mushrooms" in your journal. Are they good or bad for people? (Remember that you can check off more than one column.)

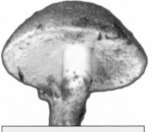

WARNING:
UNLESS YOU ARE WITH AN EXPERT, DO NOT COLLECT MUSHROOMS FOR EATING! ALTHOUGH MANY TYPES ARE EDIBLE, MANY OTHERS ARE POISONOUS. LEAVE THE MUSHROOM GATHERING TO AN ADULT, WHO CAN EASILY PICK SOME UP AT YOUR LOCAL GROCERY STORE.

o b s e r v a t i o n s

• In a place that is sheltered from wind, remove the stem from a mushroom and flip over its cap. See the interesting layers underneath the cap? These are called gills, and they look almost like the gills of a fish. The gills hold the mushroom's spores.

- Place the cap of the mushroom (with the gills facing down) on a page from a self-sticking photo album (pull back the protective covering first). Cover the mushroom cap with a bowl overnight. When you return and remove the bowl and mushroom cap, you'll see a wonderful pattern of spores on the album page. Draw a picture of this pattern in your journal, and then try the experiment again using different types of mushrooms. Are the patterns always the same?

This mushroom popped up in a newly planted vegetable garden.

explanation

Just like people, fungi have numerous differences. They come in many different sizes, but they all have one thing in common: Spores spread them. The smaller the fungus, the more difficult it is to see its spores.

Different types of mushrooms have different patterns of gills and different colors of spores. If you don't trap the spores on something sticky, they will travel off into the air and land just about everywhere. If conditions are right (warm and damp), a mushroom can appear within days.

Luckily for us, very few of the countless spores from all the hundreds of thousands of kinds of fungi ever actually take root and grow. If they did, the whole world might be buried in fungi. Spores of all sorts are floating in the air right now, just waiting to find a home and start growing.

conclusion

There's a big fungal world out there just waiting to be explored. Mother Nature has seen to it that billions upon billions of fungal spores get released, knowing that only a fraction of them will land on favorable surfaces (like rotting wood for mushrooms, or milk for cheese molds). Some are good and some are bad, but always know there is fungus among us!

you're being told to grow mold

INTRODUCTION

There is a whole world of microorganisms right under your nose. One of the easiest to recognize is mold, a type of fungus. Don't let your parents throw out that old loaf of bread! You have a living laboratory right in your own kitchen.

Take a look at moldy bread.

materials

Old loaf of bread
**Magnifying glass or stereo
    binocularscope**
Journal and pencil

what to do

1. Ask your parents for an old loaf of bread.
2. Let the bread sit in the bread's plastic bag for about a week in an area that is room temperature.
3. Once the bread has developed mold, take out a piece of the moldy bread and examine it with a magnifying glass (or better yet, with a stereo binocularscope).

4. Draw a picture of the mold in your journal. Date and label your drawing, using the scientific name of the mold, *Aspergillus niger*, to identify it.
5. After three days, examine the same piece of bread, checking to see if the mold has spread. Return the examined piece of moldy bread to the bread's plastic bag. Be sure to place it exactly where you found it in the loaf.

o b s e r v a t i o n s
- How many days did it take for the mold to appear?
- Did the mold have an odor?
- How quickly did the mold spread?
- Where did the mold come from?

e x p l a n a t i o n

Aspergillus niger is very easy to culture. All you need is a moist surface of nonliving organic matter. Bread fits the bill perfectly, which is why *Aspergillus niger* is commonly known as bread mold. Mold spores are everywhere, just waiting to find a friendly environment so they can do their thing.

Once spores land on the right kind of surface, they form the main body of the mold, called the mycelium. This is a mass buildup of hyphae (like a superhighway of threadlike branches). The mold must anchor itself into the bread, and does so by creating another grouping of hyphae called rhizoids. The rhizoids act as the stomach of the mold, secreting enzymes that break down the bread into a substance that can be digested for its sugars and starches. The rhizoids also absorb water, which every living organism needs to live.

But hyphae don't stop their work just yet. They also build themselves into another structure called a sporangiophore. This is a fancy word for a spore factory. Remember those spores that are floating in the air all around you, existing as if by magic? They had to have come from somewhere, and they did—from sporangiophores.

Lots of mold.

Notice the long stringlike structure called *hyphae*.

conclusion

That's a lot of big fancy words for a mold you can hardly see. But even in the smallest forms of life, intricate processes are occurring all the time. If common bread mold has so many fancy words associated with it, just imagine how complicated the processes that occur in your body are! There's a whole world of microbiology out there, just waiting for you to explore.

troubleshooting

Very few people are lucky enough to own a binocularscope, but finding one to look through may not be as hard as you might think. Most schools have a couple of binocularscopes that can be signed out by teachers for projects just like this one. Another great resource is your local Cooperative Extension Service, where binocularscopes are used daily to look for pest and disease problems. Your local Extension agent can show you many other interesting things to view under a binocularscope as well. Visiting your Cooperative Extension Service is free, and the people who work there are friendly—so what are you waiting for?

Moldy ricotta cheese.

is a dead tree really dead?

INTRODUCTION

When a tree is dead or dying, adults are often quick to cut it up and remove it. But let's take a closer look at a dead tree, to see if there might be some reasons for leaving it alone.

materials

- **Lawn chair**
- **Medium-sized screwdriver**
- **Newspaper**
- **Tweezers**
- **Magnifying glass**
- **Glass jar**
- **Field guide to insects**
- **Journal and pencil**

Find a dead tree.

Take a closer look.

what to do

1. Find a fallen tree (or tree stump) to observe.
2. Set up your lawn chair within 10 feet of the tree, so you are close enough to observe both it and its surroundings. During different times of the day, sit in the chair for a while and record in your journal any signs of life you see.
3. Using a screwdriver, dig into the decaying wood and look for insects. For best results in capturing a large variety of critters, sift through the rotted wood chunks on top of newspaper. Use tweezers to place any goodies you find in a glass jar.
4. Observe your specimens with a magnifying glass and draw pictures of them in your journal. Using a field guide to insects, try to identify them by name. When you are done, release your specimens back onto the tree.

Look for life-forms.

observations

- Was the level of activity around the tree varied at different times of the day?
- How does the decaying wood feel different from that of a living tree?
- How many different specimens were you able to find?
- Have you ever seen a tree that looks dead in one section and alive in another?

explanation

The results of your observations can vary greatly depending on your surrounding environment. The more natural the setting for the dead tree, the more likely you are to find a wide diversity of biological activity. The age of the dead tree will also affect the amount of activity around that tree.

A tree is like any other living thing: It has a life cycle. When a tree dies, microbes present in the wood help with the decomposition process. As the dead tree slowly changes back into compost, a whole world of activity is at work within. The microbes feed on the wood, which breaks down. Some insects feed on the microbes, while others just find the tree a great place to live. These insects can become food for birds and larger animals such as raccoons. But such larger animals probably won't come near the tree you're observing—at least not while you're there. Animals are instinctively cautious around humans and will stay away until you leave.

Sometimes you'll see a standing tree that has large holes in its trunk, with lots of rotting wood inside the holes. You might naturally think such a tree is dead. But don't forget to look up and check for leaves. Some trees are damaged by lightning or disease yet still survive. As long as there is a length of undisturbed bark from the ground to the branches, there is a chance that some of the tree will still leaf out and grow. The rest of the tree can become living quarters for animals.

Although this tree looks dead, one side has leaves that sprout each year.

conclusion

Although something may look dead on the outside, there is probably a lot of life within. A dead tree can mean so much to so many creatures. It can act as a source of food for microbes and insects—important members of the food chain. Encourage adults to leave dead-looking trees and tree stumps alone (of course, standing dead trees in danger of falling on people, houses, cars, and so forth should be removed).

Ants on a dead tree.

mean, mean ethylene

INTRODUCTION

Ethylene is a valuable by-product of natural gas. It has many good uses, including as an anesthetic. Although ethylene does some good for people, it can also do some damage to our friends in the plant world. Try this fun, easy, and smelly experiment to prove the point that ethylene can be mean.

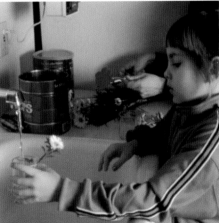

Sort into two bouquets and add water.

materials

- Two small pieces of Oasis (optional)
- One small, bunch of freshly cut flowers
- Two small plastic cups
- Package of soluble flower preservative (optional)
- Two coffee cans with lids
- Piece of ripe to overripe fruit (bananas seem to work best)
- Journal and pencil

what to do

1. Soak the Oasis in water and cut it to fit into the plastic cups.
2. Cut the stems of the flowers so they will fit inside the coffee cans when the lids are in place.
3. Double-check to make sure the bouquets are identical, and put each into a cup.

Make a journal.

4. Mix flower preservative into water (follow instructions on the package) and add the mixture to the bouquet cups.
5. Place each bouquet cup inside a coffee can.
6. Place the piece of fruit in one of the coffee cans, and then seal both cans with their lids.
7. Place the cans in a brightly lighted area near a window, but not in direct sunlight. (The closed coffee cans will heat up if placed in direct sunlight, so be careful not to let this happen.)
8. Each day over a two-week period, compare the two bouquets. Record your observations in your journal. (Both bouquets will benefit from the little bit of fresh air that comes into the cans during observation.) Replace the lids as soon as your observations are complete.
9. When finished with the experiment, promptly throw the flower bouquets and rotten fruit into the nearest compost pile. Everyone within smelling distance will thank you for it.

Place flowers in two cans.

Add overripe fruit to one can.

observations
- As the first week progressed, what did you notice happening to the petals of the flowers in the test bouquet?
- At the end of the two-week period, which bouquet was in worse shape?

explanation
Ethylene gas is released when fruit begins to rot. If this occurs in an open, well-ventilated environment, no problems result from the gas. By trapping the gas in the coffee can, you can see how it damages flower petals.

On the first day of comparison, both bouquets will probably look the same. But as the first week progresses, you will notice spots forming on the petals of the flowers in the test bouquet. And by the end of the two-week period, you will see a decline in both bouquets, but the test bouquet will be in much worse shape.

If you were to visit a floral business that also delivers fruit baskets, you would notice something interesting: The fruit and the flowers are stored in different coolers to prevent just this from happening.

conclusion

As long as fruit and flowers are not stored together, ethylene is not mean at all.

Flowers after two weeks with no fruit.

PHOTOS BY ELLEN TALMAGE

Flowers after two weeks with fruit.

likable lichens

INTRODUCTION

If someone were to ask you, "Have you ever seen lichens before?" your answer should be yes. Chances are you have walked by them many times and never given them a second thought.

Lichen is unique because it isn't just one living thing but two, living together in a symbiotic relationship. A lichen is actually a fungus and an alga that have joined together into a single living organism. It begins life, grows, and reproduces as if it were a single plant. Let's see how different types of weather can affect a lichen's appearance.

Looking at lichens.

materials

Current weather reports
Piece of colorful yarn
Magnifying glass
Colored pencils
Rain gauge
Journal and pencil

what to do

1. Monitor current weather reports by radio, newspaper, the Internet, or television.
2. During a dry spell (a week or so of dry and windy weather), go out and look for lichens on stones or trees in a shady, wooded setting.
3. When you find a lichen, mark its location by tying a piece of yarn near the specimen, so you will know where to find it later.
4. Draw a picture of the lichen in your journal, using the magnifying glass to get a better view of your specimen.
5. Color the drawing using colored pencils. Try to match the shades you see on the lichen as closely as possible with the colored pencils.
6. After a hard rain (at least ½ inch according to a rain gauge), revisit your lichen specimen.
7. Draw another picture of the lichen, on a different page of your journal, and color the drawing. Try to match the shades you see on the lichen as closely as possible.

Did you notice any change in color after a rain?

observations

• Compare the picture you drew of the lichen during dry, windy weather to the picture you drew after the rainy period. Was there a change in color?

explanation

Mother Nature has seen to it that an alga and a fungus can come together in a symbiotic relationship. Each could not live without the other. The alga helps by providing the food and water for the lichen through photosynthesis. If the alga were to live on a rock or tree trunk by itself, it would die because it is too delicate to survive long periods of dry, windy weather. The fungus, on the other hand, is a tougher organism and doesn't mind dry, windy weather at all. But the problem the fungus has is that its cells contain no chlorophyll, so it cannot make its own food.

During periods of dry weather, the fungus provides protection for the delicate alga, which actually hides behind the fungus. With the alga concealed, the lichen takes on the color of the fungus. In return for this protection, the alga gladly provides the fungus with the food it needs.

After a hard rain, when the environment is better suited for the alga, it comes out from behind the fungus. During these periods of damp weather, the lichen takes on a different coloring, resembling that of the alga. Because algae come in many different colors, don't be surprised if some lichens have a pinkish or reddish tint to them in damp weather.

conclusion

Even the smallest organisms can be fascinating. Because lichens grow only a fraction of an inch per year, people often do not notice them. Lichens are a perfect example of how living things can work together to survive.

It is interesting to note that although lichens live on rocks and tree trunks, areas that would be tough going for many creatures, they do not do well in areas where there is air pollution. And so lichens are also an example of how living things can be both tough and fragile at the same time.

Lichens covering a tree trunk.

Projects for Fun

making a living doll

INTRODUCTION

"You're a living doll." Ever hear anyone say that? It's a really old expression that you might still hear when watching an old black-and-white movie. Let's take that old expression and turn it into an experiment. Not only is this experiment fun, but you'll end up with a cute gift for a special person.

materials

Two 4-inch pots (preferably without drainage holes)

½ cup of small pebbles

Potting soil

Two small plastic dolls, less than 6 inches tall, from a craft store

Grass seed

Scissors

Index card

Journal and pencil

All the makings for a living doll.

what to do

1. Pour the pebbles evenly into the two pots.
2. Pour ½ cup of potting soil into each pot.

3. Place a doll in each pot, centering the doll and backfilling the pot with soil until just the head of the doll is showing. (Most dolls from craft stores don't have any clothes on, so they'll appreciate being covered with soil!)

4. Sprinkle lots of grass seed onto the soil and doll hair in both pots.

5. Water one of the pots well, making sure that all the soil is saturated. Pour off any excess water by tipping the pot into a sink.

Add soil and the doll so its head sticks out above the soil.

6. Place both pots in a sunny windowsill and record the planting date in your journal.

7. Compare the two pots each day and record your observations in your journal. Make sketches showing where the grass seedlings sprout and how their growth progresses.

8. Check the watered pot every couple of days, adding water as needed to keep the soil moist. Make sure the soil does not dry out.

9. Trim the grass as needed with scissors. (The doll's face should always be clear of grass, so he or she can see out!) In your journal, record the date when you first trim the grass; this trimming information will be an important part of the care instructions for your future gift.

10. On an index card, make a sign for your gift that reads:

Dear [person getting the gift]:

You're a Living Doll!

Love always,
[your name]

On the back of the index card, write a set of instructions telling the person who will receive your gift how to care for a "living doll." Be sure to include watering and trimming instructions. (You should have all the information you need in your journal.) Mowing the lawn will never be as much fun as this!

Sprinkle the grass with seed.

observations

- Did you notice any grass actually growing from the head of the "living doll"?
- What happened after about six weeks? Did the grass continue to look healthy?
- Can you think of a really easy way to replace this gift after a few weeks' time?

explanation

Grass seed is very easy to grow, but it can only germinate if it gets a good soaking with water first. Grass seed that sits on a dry surface will not grow. This happens in nature all the time. Lots of plants spread their seed onto the ground, all ready to go. It just needs to wait for a rainy time of the spring or fall.

If you thought that grass was actually growing from the head of your "living doll," poke around with a pencil near the soil line in the pot and try to determine if one or more of the grass seedlings might have grown up through the hair. It's likely that the grass you

After the grass has grown, trim the hair.

thought was growing out of the doll's head actually has its roots in the soil, in which case you've been tricked by an optical illusion.

Compare the dolls.

It's too bad that the doll didn't actually have grass growing out of its head, but there wasn't enough moisture for that to happen. Most doll hair is made from nylon, which is a material that does not absorb water. Even though you may have watered the doll's head faithfully, the hair did not absorb the water, and so the seed could not germinate there.

You will find that the grass looked its best between three and four weeks after being planting and watered. After six weeks, the grass gets crowded and the soil needs fertilizer. Why not water your other "living doll" (still "nonliving" at this point) and give that as a replacement gift to the same person a few weeks later? It's all ready to go—just add water.

After the second "living doll" is growing nicely, you may want to start over with the first by changing its soil and adding fresh seed. By using pots with drainage pebbles instead of pots with drainage holes, your "living dolls" are safe to place on desks and other furniture that might get ruined by dripping water.

A living doll!

conclusion

Seeds will remain seeds unless they are given an environment favorable for germination. Without water, grass seed can sit around for a long time without ever growing. Without the help of an indoor gardener the living dolls won't last long. These gifts will need sunlight, trimming, watering, and fertilizing or they will not thrive.

growing rainbows

INTRODUCTION

Life would be boring without color. Colors attract attention and encourage feelings of cheerfulness. Create a little colorful magic with a box of food coloring and some celery.

materials

- **Seven drinking glasses**
- **Measuring cup**
- **Small box of food coloring containing four colors (red, blue, green, and yellow)**
- **Package of celery**
- **Sharp knife**
- **Paper towels**
- **Small plate**
- **Journal and pencil**

Mix your colors.

what to do

1. Fill seven glasses with 4 ounces of water each.
2. Put 20 drops of each color into four separate glasses to make the colors red, blue, green, and yellow.
3. Put 13 drops of yellow and 7 drops of red into another glass to make the color orange.

4. Put 10 drops of blue and 3 drops of red into another glass to make the color indigo.
5. Put 10 drops of blue and 10 drops of red into the last glass to make the color violet.
6. Remove seven stalks of celery from the package. Select the younger stalks, near the center of the plant.
7. With a sharp knife, carefully cut off the bottom of each celery stalk. Do not remove any leaves from the tops of the stalks.

Arrange the celery into the colors of a rainbow— red, orange, yellow, green, blue, indigo, and violet.

8. Place a celery stalk in each of the glasses and let the stalks stand undisturbed for 24 hours.
9. Remove the celery stalks from the glasses and blot off excess water with paper towels.
10. Carefully slice off the bottom inch of each celery stalk, and then arrange the bottoms on a small plate in the order the colors appear in a rainbow: red, orange, yellow, green, blue, indigo, and violet.

observations

- What happened to the celery stalks after 24 hours?
- Were any of the colors absorbed into the celery better than others?
- Why do you think keeping the leaves on the celery stalks makes a difference in the outcome of this experiment?
- What do you think would happen if you used white flowers (roadside varieties) or an onion in this experiment?

Try white roadside flowers.

explanation

Plants cannot move around to look for their food and water like animals can. They have adapted and survived thanks to special structures that allow them to make their own food. The roots of a plant do a lot of work by absorbing minerals from soil and water into the plant itself, but then what happens?

All plants have special structures within their stems called xylem, which act like drinking straws. These structures are the pipelines that carry water and dissolved minerals up through a plant's stem and into its leaves. This movement of liquid materials from one part of a plant to another is called translocation. Leaves are an important part of this process. They actually suck up the water through the stem.

conclusion

The more leaves a celery stalk has, the more translocation occurs. In other words, the more leaves a celery stalk has, the better it sucks up colored water. Some colors are more visible than others. Although the yellow did get absorbed into the celery, it is not as visible against the light green background of the celery. The darker colors give the most contrast to the natural color of the celery, and so are more visible.

Try using white flowers to see if your results are different than the wildflowers.

making plant fossils

Flatten the clay.

INTRODUCTION

Did you ever wonder what it would have been like living thousands or even millions of years ago? Paleontologists have learned what they know through studying fossils. Some of the plants and animals of long ago died and sank into the mud at the bottoms of lakes. Slowly the dead plants and animals were covered with more mud, which protected them from the elements. Thousands of years went by, and eventually this growing pile of mud turned into stone, creating stone copies of the plants and animals that had become buried there. In many parts of the world, the rocks containing these copies—fossils—have been pushed up toward the surface of the earth, where the fossils can be more easily uncovered.

Select fern fronds.

It's fun and easy to make exact replicas of plants using self-hardening clay. Let's make a fossil necklace using a variety of plant materials that would have been eaten by an old extinct relative of the elephant.

materials

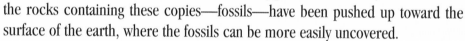

Plastic bag for gathering plant
  materials

Newspaper

Clay (nontoxic, self-hardening)

Rolling pin or drinking glass

Coffee-can lid (optional)

Table knife

Rawhide shoelace

Twist ties

Silk flowers (optional)

Journal and pencil

what to do

1. Gather plant materials (fern fronds, pinecones, pine needles, grasses).
2. Pinch off a portion of clay to make a ball about 2 inches in diameter.
3. On newspaper, flatten the ball of clay using either a rolling pin or a drinking glass turned on its side. The flattened piece of clay should be about ¼ inch thick.
4. Place the coffee-can lid over the flattened clay and trim the clay into a circle using a table knife. (Skip this step if you want your fossil pendant to have a rougher, more natural edge.)
5. Select a nice fern frond and lay it (top side facing up) in the middle of the flattened clay.
6. Using the rolling pin or drinking glass, press the frond into the clay.
7. Remove the frond slowly and carefully to leave a clear imprint in the clay.
8. Using a pencil, punch a hole in what will be the top edge of the clay pendant, and let the pendant dry undisturbed for 48 hours.
9. String the pendant onto the rawhide shoelace and attach several pinecones on either side of the pendant using twist ties.
10. If you want to decorate your necklace further, attach pine needles, grasses, and silk flowers. Twist a tie snugly around the end of a cluster of pine needles, grasses, or silk flowers, leaving the ends of the tie open. Use the ends of the tie to attach the cluster to the necklace. Add more clusters as desired.
11. Put on your necklace and pretend that you are a woolly mammoth by swinging your large trunk and showing off your tusks. You'll already have your lunch packed for the day in the form of a lovely fossil necklace.

Press the fern fronds into the clay.

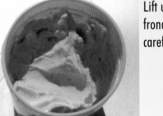

Lift up the frond carefully.

observations

- You may have noticed that brownish red dots were deposited into the clay. These dots are the fern's spores, and are found on the back of the frond. If paleontologists were to discover your fossil necklace hundreds of years from now, how might these spores be of interest to them? Record your thoughts in your journal.

- Can you think of anything else that paleontologists might be able to learn about the world you live in now by examining your fossil necklace hundreds of years in the future? Record your thoughts.

String up silk flowers.

explanation

Primitive plants like ferns use spores instead of seeds to reproduce. Paleontologists can learn a great deal by studying spores and seeds from plants of the past. By comparing them to spores and seeds of today, paleontologists can determine how and if plants have changed over time. How do we know that the items on your necklace are the ancient food of the mammoths? The answer is fascinating! When a frozen mammoth was discovered in the frozen tundra in Siberia, scientists cut open its stomach and found the remains of ferns, pinecones, pine needles, flowers, and grasses.

Display your creation.

conclusion

Things that we use every day in our lives (things that may not even be special to us) become tomorrow's prized artifacts.

make an impression with pressed flowers

INTRODUCTION

Ever wish that you could save a nice day forever? Although it is impossible to save time, it is possible to save some of the lovely flowering plants that you encounter while exploring.

Pick some flowers.

materials

Self-sticking mailing labels

Small safety pins

Two bath towels

Paper towels

Large, old phone book or flower press

Sink

Heavy card-stock paper (sized to fit your journal)

Clear tape

Ruler

Hole punch

Page protectors

Field guide to local wildflowers or gardening books

Permanent marker

Journal and pencil

what to do

1. Go out into your yard or out onto the nearest nature trail and collect up to 12 flowering plant specimens. (Be sure to obtain any necessary permissions—see "Troubleshooting" on pg.55.)

2. In your journal (in pencil), enter a brief numbered description of each plant specimen and where you found it. Also, guess the name of the plant. You may find it helpful to measure the size of the flower with a ruler. Bloom size may be a useful clue for the identification process. (For example, "Specimen #1: Yellow flower, 1 inch wide. This plant was growing in a shady place in very wet soil. Identification: Daisy.")

3. When you have finished the collection process, spread out the towel in a shady spot (if possible) that is also protected from the wind. Fold the towel lengthwise and lay out your specimens.

4. Carefully pin a mailing label to the towel next to each plant (don't remove the backings from the labels). On each label, write (in pencil) the specimen number, its name (your best guess), and the date of collection. (By adding the date, you will know the age of the preserved specimens and have a visual diary of your special day of exploration.)

5. Write a description of the specimen in the corner of the mailing label (in light pencil) to help distinguish each specimen from another.

6. Carefully roll up the towel (rolling your specimens inside the towel) and take it inside to a sink.

7. Unroll the towel and rinse off your specimens to remove any dirt and insects that might be hidden in the leaves.

8. Put the damp plants back onto the towel next to their respective labels. Blot off any excess water with paper towels.

9. Transfer your specimens and labels to a fresh, dry towel and allow them to air-dry for a few hours. (Be sure to place this towel in an area that has plenty of air circulation. If flowering plants are pressed when they are too wet, their petals will get moldy.)

Pick some more.

Choose another kind.

10. Lay out specimens for pressing one at a time on pages of an open phone book or on the special blotter paper supplied with a flower press. Arrange the leaves and flowers of each specimen so they do not overlap and also so they mimic the natural appearance of the plant. Finally, place the specimen's label beside it.

11. After laying out each specimen, cover it by closing a stack of phone-book pages (at least ⅛ inch thick) on top of the specimen, or by covering it with more blotter paper. Blotter paper absorbs more water than the paper in the phone book, so you don't need so many sheets.

Use absorbent paper to absorb the moisture from the plant.

12. When all specimens have been laid out inside the phone book or between sheets of blotter paper, move the phone book or flower press to a warm, dry area. If using a phone book, place a heavy object on top of it to help flatten the pages evenly over the flowers.

A plant press.

13. Check your specimens after three days. If the pages seem damp, reposition the specimens on drier pages.

14. After two to three weeks, the drying period should be complete. Remove the pressed plants and mount each specimen on its own sheet of heavy card-stock paper, using clear tape to fasten the flattened plant to the paper in several places along the stem. Peel off the backing of the specimen's mailing label and attach the label to the page.

Arrange the flowers.

15. Punch holes in the card stock and insert the specimen pages into page protectors and then into your journal. (Be sure to store your journal in an area that is warm and dry when it is not in use, so that the pressed plants will last for many years. At botanical gardens, the herbariums are carefully monitored to make sure their preserved specimens stay warm and dry, so you should do the same.)

16. Now is the time to double-check your detective work. Using a field guide to wildflowers, gardening books, or

(better yet) the help of an experienced gardener, try to identify the plant specimens you have collected. Erase your penciled-in guesses from your journal and from the specimen labels and write (in permanent marker) the correct name for each plant. (If you choose to write the scientific names of your specimens, use the following format: Genus species. The first word—the genus—starts with a capital letter, and the second word—the species—starts with a lowercase letter.)

Use an old phone book.

observations

- Do the dried specimens look as good as the plants did when you collected them? How are they different?
- Review your journal notes about the growing conditions in which you found your specimens. How do you think these conditions are related to the success of your pressings?
- If you were unable to positively identify any of your specimens through observation and research, just put question marks on their labels and in your journal notes. Maybe you'll find their names in years to come.

Use a heavy object.

explanation

As with all living things, plants have their differences. Some specimens will dry beautifully because they store very little water in their leaves and are better able to lie flat. Others will not dry as successfully because they naturally hold a lot of water and never seem to fully dry when using this particular pressing method.

conclusion

By making your own herbarium, you have made an impression on your mind about the plant specimens you have collected and dried.

As you rediscover your journal many years from now and look at your specimens, you will probably remember the day you collected these plants and how much fun it was pretending to be a botanist. One of the best things about making your own herbarium is that now you've got all the time you need to study and research your flowering plant specimens. If you were only able to work with fresh specimens, you would have a very limited time to study a plant because most plants flower for only a few weeks of the year.

t r o u b l e s h o o t i n g

Always ask property owners if it is okay to pick flowers from their land. If you are on a nature trail that is publicly owned, ask a park ranger whether specimens can be taken. Some plants are very rare and should never be touched (even for the sake of science) because they are endangered. If this is the case, take a picture of the plant or make a sketch instead. Although you might not have a pressed specimen of that particular plant, feel good that you were able to observe it in its natural habitat.

Before and after.

PHOTO BY
DAN GILREIN

If visiting a nature trail isn't possible, ask a gardener if you can collect specimens from his or her yard. If the gardener is experienced, ask him or her to help you figure out what treasures you have collected. Field guides to local wildflowers and gardening books from your local library will also help you determine what treasures you have collected.

building a floatarium

INTRODUCTION

If you ask a gardener to explain what a terrarium is, he or she will probably describe a small, enclosed container in which small plants and animals are grown and kept. Sometimes it's fun to do things that are a little different. Let's build a terrarium for some other very special members of the floral world, the floating plants. With this special environment, you'll be able to examine several floating plants up close and determine how each keeps its head above water.

Pour gravel into the container.

materials

- **2 cups of large gravel or fish gravel**
- **Colander**
- **Garden hose with spray nozzle**
- **2-gallon storage container made of clear plastic**
- **Paper towels**
- **Liquid fertilizer and fertilizer tablets**
- **Submerged, oxygenating plant**
- **Spoon**
- **Floating aquatic plants**
- **Snail(s)**
- **Journal and pencil**

Add water.

what to do

1. Outside, pour the gravel into the colander and rinse with the hose to remove any excess dirt and salts that might cloud the water. (If you are using commercial gravel, this step is not necessary.)
2. Moisten a paper towel and wipe out any dust that may have accumulated inside the plastic container.
3. Pour the rinsed gravel into the container and then add water, filling the container until it is two-thirds full.
4. Break off an appropriately sized portion of a fertilizer tablet (follow directions on the package) and bury it in the gravel.
5. Anchor the oxygenating plant in the gravel so that it is positioned on top of the fertilizer tablet. Using the spoon, dig a hole near the fertilizer tablet and move the rubber-banded part of the oxygenating plant back and forth until it is resting on the bottom of the plastic container. Mound up gravel around the plant to make sure it stays in place.
6. Place various floating plants (see "Observations" below) on the surface of the water.
7. Add liquid fertilizer to your floatarium (follow directions on the package).
8. Finally, add a snail or two to your floatarium.

Bury the stems of the *Elodea* plant.

Add floating plants.

observations

- Duckweed (*Lemna minor*) is a tiny plant that sticks to the surface of the water. It sticks so well, in fact, that you might get a little nervous about it. Stick your finger into the floatarium and see what happens. Now that you've got duckweed on your finger, try to get it off. (Don't get too alarmed; it rinses off easily with water.) Place a couple of these plants in your journal and let them dry. You'll see that they are harmless when dried.
- Parrot feather (*Myriophyllum brasiliense*) is a floating plant that always

seems to find its proper place in the world. It sticks its green leaves above the waterline to absorb the sunlight it requires to grow. The underwater leaves yellow out and eventually break off, and a thin root system grows out of the bottom of the submerged stem. If you pluck off the top of a parrot feather and float it by itself in the floatarium, you'll notice that it floats in a similar fashion. Although it may take a week or so to adjust, you'll soon find that roughly half of the leaves stay above the waterline while the rest stay underwater. Make some sketches in your journal to record how long it takes for a new root system to form. Congratulations, you have just hatched a new parrot feather!

Duckweed.

- Floating fern (*rotundifolia*) is a plant that is fun to touch. It is about the size of a fingernail and is very soft. Because it is small, it can float on top of the water with little trouble. Before you place your soft little friends in the floatarium, make a note in your journal as to how many there are. In a month's time, go back and count the number now present in the floatarium. Has the number stayed the same, or has there been some growth? Old floating ferns will eventually die off and rot, providing a natural source of fertilizer for the water.

Floating fern.

- Water lettuce (*Pistia stratiotes*) is really easy to grow and readily available in pet shops. It's hard to believe that a plant that can get as large as a grapefruit can actually float. Water lettuce is so good at floating that you can't keep it underwater, even if you try. Push some water lettuce to the bottom of your floatarium, upside down, and watch what happens. It will pop up to the surface and float right-side up each and every time. Ask friends to try to sink the water lettuce. Tell them it's a game. Write down their results in your journal. When they want to know why they float, open up a leaf and show them the air chambers.

Elodea.

PHOTO BY
DAN
GILREIN

- With all this floating fun going on, you'll want to make sure that the water in your floatarium stays nice and clear. To do this, add some waterweed (a submergent plant of the genus *Elodea canadensis*) to the party. *Elodea* provides a nice, comfortable home for snails, but they don't eat it. Snails are great scavengers, so when you provide a good home for them, they in turn will clean the inside walls of your floatarium by eating the algae that form there. Without snails, the algae could eventually become so thick that they block your view into the floatarium.

Pushing under water lettuce.

explanation

Duckweed's ability to stick to surfaces is what enables it to move from one place to another. If you happen to accidentally pick up some duckweed hitchhikers from the pet store (duckweed often attaches itself to other water plants), you'll soon have a permanent colony of these little ducklings in your floatarium. But there is a very simple way to control duckweed: Let the little ducklings dry out and they will vanish.

Parrot feather probably gets disturbed quite a lot in its natural environment. High wind and waves during bad weather constantly upset the balance of this delicate plant. But because parrot feather has the ability to stay afloat and make new roots when broken, it continues to thrive, particularly in a warm, freshwater environment.

It floats.

Trying to accurately count a large population of floating ferns can be a difficult task. You might try pushing those plants that have been counted into one corner of the floatarium, so they don't get recounted. To do this, use a piece of cardboard sized almost as wide as the floatarium, and herd the floating ferns behind it once they have been counted.

The secret to the success of water lettuce lies in the leaves themselves. Gently tear open a big leaf and examine it. Notice all those air spaces inside the leaf? The leaves of this plant act like little lungs, helping to keep it afloat. Have you ever noticed that when floating in a pool, keeping your lungs filled with air helps you stay on the surface of the water? And that exhaling the air from your lungs makes you sink? A life preserver works on the same principle

Look at the air pockets.

(air causes buoyancy). Even though water lettuce is very big compared to floating ferns and duckweed, its leaves are always filled with air, so it stays afloat easily. No matter how many times you try to sink it, it will always rise to the surface.

Water lettuce.

conclusion

Congratulations! You have just built your very own ecosystem. Your floatarium represents submerged and floating members of the plant family.

Now you know firsthand what it means to move at a snail's pace! Snails are slow to get where they are going. But in this case, we don't need them to be speedy. We just want them to eat some algae along the way—and to be happy in this wonderful habitat called a floatarium.

Parrot feather.

CAUTION:
WATER PLANTS GROWN IN FLOATARIUMS SHOULD *NOT* BE RELEASED OUTSIDE IN NATURAL WATERWAYS. THEY COULD TAKE OVER THE EXISTING PLANT COMMUNITIES.

what makes a good soil?

INTRODUCTION

Did you ever wonder if plants could grow in different media? Can bean seeds be fooled into sprouting, even if they are not planted in the ground? In this experiment we will try to grow bean seeds in six types of media. By keeping a visual record, you will be able to track the effectiveness of each type of medium and decide what makes a good soil.

materials

- Six plastic drinking cups
- 3 x 5–inch sponge
- Scissors
- Bean seeds (any variety)
- Rubber band
- Rubber gloves
- ⅓ cup colorful fish gravel
- ⅓ cup sand
- ⅓ cup dirt
- ⅓ cup commercial potting soil
- ⅓ cup coffee grounds (after brewing)
- Six plastic garden markers
- 13 x 9–inch foil baking pan
- Journal and pencil

Dig up some dirt.

Use a pencil to gently dig holes for the bean seeds.

Let the tests begin!

1. Poke three holes in the bottom of each cup using the tip of a pencil.

2. Cut the sponge (the first medium) in half so each piece measures 3 x 2½ inches. Soak the sponge pieces in warm tap water and let drain.

3. Place two bean seeds between the sponge pieces, bind the sponge pieces together with a rubber band, and place the bound sponge pieces in one of the cups.

4. Pour half of the five remaining media (fish gravel, sand, dirt, potting soil, coffee grounds) into the five remaining cups (one medium per cup). Moisten any media that are overly dry by gradually adding a few drops of water until they are moist.

5. For each of these five cups, make a 1-inch hole in its medium by inserting a pencil and gently wiggling it back and forth. Place two bean seeds in the hole and pour the rest of the appropriate medium into the cup.

6. Write the date on one side of each garden marker, and the type of medium on the other side. Place each marker in its appropriate cup.

7. Water each of the five remaining cups with up to ⅓ cup of water, making sure to water the medium slowly and evenly over its entire surface. If the medium becomes fully saturated before the ⅓ cup of water is gone, discard the extra water.

Coffee grounds get moldy and smelly in a week's time.

Beans grow, but don't thrive.

8. Let the cups stand in the sink for about five minutes, and then place them in a foil baking pan and move them to a sunny windowsill.

9. Check on your experiment every day to make sure the media stay moist. The amount of water required will vary with each medium.

10. Create a "What Makes Good Soil" worksheet to record your observations every three to four days. The exact number of days for germination will vary depending on the type of bean seeds you use, but you can start to look for seedlings about 10 days after planting. For each medium, be sure to record when the bean seeds sprout (or if they sprout at all). Throw out any flops before they start to smell too bad, and transplant successes into larger pots if you want to keep them.

Add needed nutrients.

observations
- For which medium did germination begin first?
- For which media did germination fail?
- For the media that produced germination, did the bean plants remain healthy?

explanation
Now that you know which of the test media are best for growing bean plants, let's dig a little deeper into the science of soil and figure out why some of the media did not work at all. In order for plants to grow well, they need to have fresh air, sun, water, and soil. The soil is a place that anchors the roots and offers protection from sunlight. The soil also acts as a grocery store for the plant, providing it with the nutrients essential for its growth. Nitrogen (N), phosphorus (P), and potash (K) are the most important nutrients. Just as we humans need vitamins, minerals, and food to grow and stay healthy, plants need their nutrients.

The next time you are in a hardware store or garden center, read the label on a bag of fertilizer. Each of the letters N, P, and K will be represented by numbers, along with the various levels of these nutrients present in that particular fertilizer. (Example: A bag showing 5-10-3 means there are 5 parts N to 10 parts P to 3 parts K.) By choosing fertilizers with higher levels of certain nutrients, you can change how a plant responds. Nitrogen gives plants their dark green colors and aids in the growth of stems and leaves. Phosphorus is the most important nutrient for root formation. And potash stimulates flowering and makes fruits and vegetables tastier by converting sunlight into starches and sugars.

Use natural fertilizers such as woodchips.

Before planting in early spring, it is important to test your soil to determine its current levels of N-P-K. Good gardeners adjust accordingly and do not add fertilizer if it is not needed. And not all fertilizer needs to come in powdered form from a garden center. You can always amend the soil with organic fertilizers such as leaf litter, aged manure, or compost from your backyard.

Soil test kits are available in many stores and are reasonably priced.

It is also important to check the pH of your soil. A pH test simply tells you if your soil is too acidic (a low pH) or too alkaline (a high pH) for plant growth. Some plants grow better when the soil is more acidic, while others grow better when the soil is more alkaline. Bean seeds grow best in soil that has a pH between 6.0 and 7.5 (right in the middle, on a scale from 0 to 14). Most plants do well in this range because a soil with a middle pH makes most nutrients easily available to a plant's roots. If the pH is too high or too low, the nutrients bind up and are not available for the plant's use.

To test the soil, crumble lumps of dirt into a fine powder and follow the test kit directions.

conclusion

Any seed that is given moisture, warmth, and darkness can germinate. Regardless of soil conditions, a seed first lives off of its endosperm and can survive until this food supply is used up. After that, when the seed has become a seedling, the plant must rely on its newly formed roots, which gather up the food and water it needs from the soil. If the soil is lacking at this point, the seedling will fail. This is when you can really tell which of the media you tested make for a good soil. Although all the media tested can physically hold up the bean plants, those that supply real nourishment and water-holding capacity are the ones that make the best homes for growing bean plants.

The water above the soil is poured into special test vials, specialized color capsules are added to the vial. The results are based on the color chart provided on the side of the vial.

Watering these different media is an art. Don't be surprised if some media hold a lot of moisture and rarely need watering, while other media need watering every day. If for some reason a medium seems unable to drain its water, you may need to repunch the holes in the bottom of its cup. Standing water is not a good environment for bean seeds. They can actually drown if they sit too long in water.

The bean seeds planted in the fish gravel will often rise to the top of their container when watered with a heavy stream of water. If this should happen, try to reposition the seeds using the tip of a pencil. The bean seeds planted in the sponge pieces may require a different type of watering altogether. If the sponge pieces happen to dry out, place them (still bound together) in a bowl of cool water and allow them to soak up water. Squeeze out the excess water and return them to their cup.

Note that the bean seeds planted in the coffee grounds will probably start to mold after about two weeks. They should be thrown out when this happens.

Roots don't like sunlight so they will not leave the darkness of their soil.

Order polymer soils to amaze your friends. Plants can live in the colorful gels for months.

Critters

raising painted ladies

INTRODUCTION

For most people, butterflies are without question the most beautiful of all insects. Besides being pleasant to look at, butterflies help many flowering plants produce their seeds. When a butterfly drinks the nectar from a flower, it spreads the pollen from one plant to another. The mixings of pollens is what cause plants to reproduce.

Did you know that some butterflies can actually be raised right in your home or classroom? *Vanessa cardui* is the scientific name for the butterflies we will be raising in this project. They are commonly known as painted ladies because of all the beautiful patterns on their wings. Building a hatchery for painted ladies is simple and fun to do!

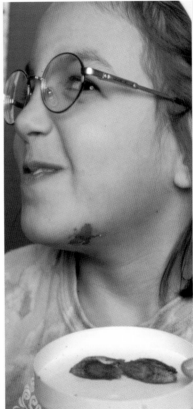

Showing chrysalises what they will look like with a temporary tattoo.

materials

Painted lady butterfly kit

Large aquarium

Yellow or white paper (enough to cover the bottom and backside of the aquarium)

Roll of aluminum screening

Paper clips

Scissors

Tape

Measuring cup

Measuring spoons

Sugar or honey

Paper towels or sponge

Small drinking glass or shallow dish

Journal and pencil

what to do

1. Order a painted lady butterfly kit through your school. When you receive the kit, record the arrival date in your journal and unpack the kit immediately.

2. Remove the plastic jar that contains the larvae (caterpillars) and place it in an area that is out of direct sunlight and protected from extreme heat or cold. Notice that there are air holes punched in the lid of the container and a piece of tissue paper just below the lid. Do not disturb the larvae by opening the lid. The green paste at the bottom of the cup is the larvae's food.

3. Every day or two, observe the larvae to see if they are getting any bigger and record your observations in your journal.

4. There is nothing else to do but wait for the first big change—metamorphosis. When it happens, record the date of this event in your journal. (Normally it should take between five and ten days for the caterpillars to turn into chrysalises, but it can take longer.)

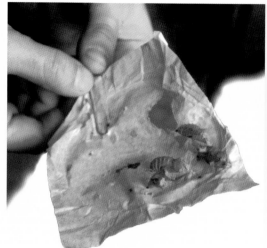

Examine the reddish liquid on the tissue paper from the hatched butterflies's wings.

Notice how the chrysalises attach themselves to the tissue paper.

Preparing the Hatchery

1. Cover the back and bottom of the aquarium with yellow or white paper. The paper's color gives a nice background for taking pictures and will make observations easier.

2. Carefully cut an 8 x 14–inch piece of aluminum screening. Roll this piece into a cylinder that is 8 inches tall. Use paper clips to fasten the screen into its cylinder configuration and place it in the center of the aquarium.

3. When the larvae turn into chrysalises, carefully remove the piece of tissue paper from their jar, which they will have fastened themselves to.

4. Use a paper clip to fasten the tissue paper to the screen cylinder. Be sure to position the tissue so that the chrysalises are facing outward and not touching the screen.

5. Position the cylinder so the tissue paper can easily be seen during the observation period.

6. Discard the kit.

7. Cut another piece of aluminum screening large enough to fit over the top of the aquarium. Tape the screen to the top of the hatchery to ensure that the adult butterflies will not fly away.

8. Once the chrysalises turn into butterflies (seven to ten days after you move them into the hatchery), prepare a homemade nectar solution to feed them. Do not touch the butterflies for at least two hours; they need this time to air-dry their wings and let them harden.

9. Once the butterflies' wings have dried, place the nectar glass in the hatchery. Gently pick up one of the butterflies and stick its feet into the feeder, so it can taste the nectar and learn that this is its food.

10. Place branches from plants of the *Malva* genus in the hatchery to encourage the egg-laying process (see "Troubleshooting" for more information on growing host plants).

11. If the weather is too cold for the newly hatched butterflies to be released outside, you can repeat another life cycle in the hatchery as long as you have the plants the larvae need to eat. Hopefully, your newly hatched butterflies will be a mixture of males and females. If this is the case, the males will mate with the females. Five to seven days after hatching, the females will then start to lay small eggs on the host plants you have provided. Three to five days later the eggs will hatch—and out pop the

A newly hatched painted lady.

Help it find food.

caterpillars. If you don't want to bother with repeating another life cycle, plan to raise the butterflies so they hatch during the frost-free season of the year, so you can release them into the great outdoors. In planning your start date, allow two to three weeks for the entire process—from ordering the butterfly kit to releasing the adult butterflies.

A painted lady tickles!

observations

- How big were the caterpillars when they arrived? How big did they get before their big change?
- Did you notice any little skins lying around as the caterpillars grew?
- As the caterpillars ate up their pasty green food, what came out of their rear ends?
- A few days before the chrysalises split open, did you notice that they began to wiggle around while still attached to the tissue paper? What do you think was happening inside the chrysalises?
- Why do you think the newly hatched butterflies flapped their wings? Did you notice any liquid on the tissue paper? What do you think this was?
- After you helped the first butterfly find the nectar, how long did it take the other butterflies to find it?
- If you completed another life cycle, answer these questions: On what part of the host plants did the females lay their eggs? What color were the eggs, and how big were they? How many days did it take the eggs to hatch?

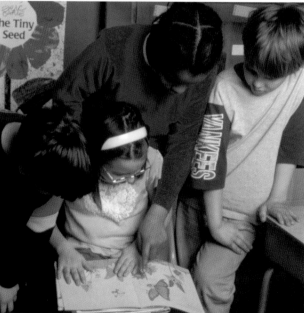

Learn more about these natural beauties in books!

You probably noticed little skins lying around the caterpillars as they grew. This is a normal process. As the larvae eat and grow, they shed their skins so their bodies can get bigger.

When the butterflies emerge from their chrysalises, the hatchlings flap their wings to help work blood through them. If you see liquid coming out of their wings, don't be nervous. A butterfly's wings have glands designed to pump liquid into the wings, which provides strength to the wings. Relax, the butterflies are not bleeding to death. There is usually more liquid in the glands than needed, so the extra drips out.

Each species has its own distinct chrysalis.

conclusion

By providing water, food, and a suitable habitat, we can raise a generation (or more) of painted ladies in a humanmade environment and experience the magic of metamorphosis firsthand. When the time comes to release your winged friends into the warm and sunny world, be sure to wave goodbye and smile. Who said learning isn't fun?

Swallowtail chrysalises.

troubleshooting
How to Get Butterfly Kits

Contact your local Cooperative Extension Service office or your school's science department to order butterfly kits. Kits may also be purchased over the Internet. Before making your purchase, closely examine any information about what the kit offers. Some kits are very pricey and give you things you really don't need. All you really need are three things: larvae, a container for the larvae, and a food source. Remember to unpack your kit immediately when you receive it.

Growing Host Plants

In planning a timeline for your hatchery, allow eight to ten weeks for the plants to germinate and grow large enough to be used as a food source.

Butterfly host plants can be grown.

Host plants can be easily grown from seed. A couple of members of the *Malva* genus are particularly easy to find. Hollyhock and mallow seeds can be found in the perennial seed racks of any garden center. In addition, fully grown plants are available in late spring. It is a good idea to have at least three plants ready for each family of butterflies you plan to raise. Once you have released your butterflies, transplant larger plants to your garden so your butterflies can visit you, and so their wild cousins can drop by as well for a meal and a place to stay.

Look at butterfly displays.

If you decide to raise another generation of painted ladies, be sure to have a good supply of fresh food for the larvae to eat. Painted ladies lay their eggs on host plants of the *Malva* genus to provide a ready source of food for the caterpillar hatchlings.

Observe by moving slowly.

Homemade Nectar Recipe

Mix a 5 percent sugar solution by adding 1 teaspoon of sugar or honey to 2 cups of warm water. Roll three paper towels together into a cylinder and fold in half. Dip this folded paper-towel roll into the solution and put it (folded end first) into a small drinking glass or shallow dish for support. Make sure the paper towels never dry out.

Another way to feed the butterflies is to soak a small piece of sponge in the sugar solution. Again, make sure the sponge never dries out. After you release your butterflies, throw away any extra solution. Always make a fresh batch for each generation of butterflies you raise.

building a worm condo

INTRODUCTION

Did you ever wonder what it looks like underground? Red worms know, and now you too can experience being underground when you build a condo for red worms. The scientific name for red worms is *Eisenia foetida*, and they are found naturally in manure and compost piles. They serve a useful role in nature by breaking down rotting vegetation and manure as they tunnel in and out of the compost they feast upon. Their tunneling also creates air spaces in the soil, which are vital for healthy plant growth. Worm poop (more politely called castings) is a great fertilizer for plants.

By building a worm condo you will be able to make a fertilizer factory. The castings will build up in the condo and can be harvested. Feed these castings to your houseplants to keep them green and healthy.

Kids can finish assembling the condo by themselves.

> ## NOTE:
> **HAVE AN ADULT HELP YOU WITH**
> **BUILDING THE WORM CONDO.**
> **SEE ILLUSTRATION ON PAGE 74**
> **FOR GUIDANCE.**

Building the Worm Condo

materials

- Two pieces of 2 x 12 x 24–inch Plexiglas
- One piece of 2 x 2 x 24–inch pressure-treated lumber
- Two pieces of 2 x 2 x 10–inch pressure-treated lumber
- Two pieces of 2 x 2 x 6–inch pressure-treated lumber
- Six ¼-inch stove bolts, 2½ inches long
- Six ¼-inch wing nuts
- Four 2½-inch Sheetrock screws
- T-square (builder's tool)
- Electric drill and bits (⅛-inch bit for Sheetrock screws; ¼-inch bit for stove bolts)
- Two old phone books

Screw in the wing nuts.

what to do

1. Screw the 2 x 2 x 6–inch cross pieces into the 2 x 2 x 24–inch base and then back out the screws and remove the crosspieces.
2. Place the two phone books on the floor so you can drill into them without damaging the floor.
3. On top of the phone books, sandwich the 2 x 2 x 24–inch piece of wood and the two 2 x 2 x 10–inch pieces of wood between the two pieces of Plexiglas.
4. Slowly and carefully drill six holes completely through all the layers of the Plexiglas/wood sandwich (don't be afraid to drill into the phone books).
5. Push the six stove bolts into the Plexiglas/wood sandwich and set it up on its end.
6. Refasten the two crosspieces to the back of the base.
7. Put the wing nuts on the bolts and tighten.

Fill the condo with paper and food scraps.

Furnishing and Populating the Worm Condo

materials

- Peat moss (about ½ pound)
- Newspaper (about ½ pound, or 25 sheets)
- Rubber gloves
- 2 or 3 handfuls of leaf mold
- 1 handful of powdered limestone
- 2 to 3 cups of fruit and vegetable scraps (you can also throw in an eggshell and 1 tablespoon of coffee grounds for good luck)
- Large pail
- ½ cup of colorful fish gravel
- ¼ pound of red worms
- Large, black plastic garbage bag
- Scissors and tape
- Long barbecue fork
- Journal and pencil

Looking for worms to move into the new condo.

what to do

1. Soak the peat moss in tepid water for 10 minutes and allow to drain.
2. Shred the newspaper into strips about 2 inches wide, soak in tepid water, and allow to drain.
3. Squeeze out any excess water from the peat moss and newspaper.
4. Combine all the ingredients (peat moss, newspaper, leaf mold, limestone, food scraps) in a large pail and mix thoroughly.
5. Pour half the soil mixture into the worm condo.
6. Sprinkle a thin layer of fish gravel about ¼ inch thick into the condo, and then add another layer of soil mixture about ½ inch thick.
7. Dump the worms into the condo (use the long fork if you are squeamish) and cover them with the rest of the soil mixture.

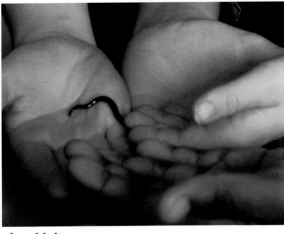

Some kids dig worms!

8. Stretch the black garbage bag tightly over the top of the condo and tape it to the frame. This cover will prevent light from entering the condo (simulating underground conditions) and will also keep the soil mixture from drying out. Remember to always keep this cover on the condo except when you want to observe the worms or feed them more food scraps.

9. Using scissors, carefully poke several holes in the plastic cover (for good air circulation) and trim off any excess plastic.

10. In your journal, record the start date for your worm condo.

11. Place the worm condo in a spot that is out of direct sunlight.

Pour the worms into their new home.

Long-Term Care of the Worm Condo

Add fruit and vegetable scraps whenever available. Using your long fork, slowly dig down

Cover with black plastic, but don't forget the air holes!

about 6 inches into the soil mixture. By digging slowly you will give the worms a chance to move out of harm's way. Place the scraps in the bedding and bury them. Be sure to add the food scraps to different sections of the condo each time you feed your worms, so you don't overly disturb them in any one area.

By the fourth month, the worms should have processed the newspaper and other ingredients and created lots of castings. You should harvest the castings at this point (and every four months after that) for use as fertilizer. Harvest up to two-thirds of the castings at a time, making sure to replace them with moistened newspaper strips and food scraps. For a 4-inch potted plant, use 1 teaspoon of castings (use more for larger plants). Store the excess castings in a sealed glass container for future use, or give them to your friends. Use the castings to fertilize your plants every one to two months.

Add a layer of peat moss to the condo mixture.

Harvest the castings.

observations

- How do the worms react when you remove the plastic cover for observation?
- What do the worms feel like when you hold them? Are they slimy like slugs, or are they dry?
- How do other people react to holding the worms?
- What happens to the rotting food scraps over time? Does the soil level change or stay the same? Do you notice any movement of the fish gravel?

explanation

Worms are very sensitive to light and will dig toward the center of the condo to avoid exposure. The trick to seeing them is to remove the plastic cover quickly, before they have a chance to tunnel into the center on their condo.

Worms bring an interesting sensation to people who hold them. Although worms have no bones, they do have a strong set of muscles, and their movements can tickle the palm of your hand. It is fascinating to watch them expand and contract in order to move about. They are not slimy like slugs, nor are they sticky. If they were, soil would stick to them and they couldn't move through it as easily as they do.

Some kids are not as fond of worms as others are. Let those who are squeamish about touching worms get accustomed to the idea by first watching or feeding them. Before you know it (and before your squeamish friends know it), they'll probably be holding the worms and actually enjoying the experience.

Use castings for fertilizer.

As the worms work their magic, digesting the rotting food scraps and turning the soil mixture, the level of the bedding may drop slightly. If so, add more food scraps and moistened newspaper strips as needed. You'll notice that the longer the worms work the soil mixture, the more the layers of the bedding get mixed together. Eventually, the fish gravel you put halfway down into the soil mixture will get mixed throughout the bedding. These colorful rocks help you see how much worms really do turn soil.

conclusion

At first you may feel a little squeamish about having worms in your home or classroom, but they are harmless, odorless, and hardworking. Red worms are easy to care for and fun to watch. During summer, when temperatures are warm enough for worms to live comfortably outdoors, you may want to transfer your pets to a compost pile in your yard. If you alternate their home back and forth between their indoor condo and an outdoor compost pile, they will get a more varied diet and be healthier. Be sure to bring them back to their condo before the first killing frost. As long as you provide a favorable place for the worms to live, you will have a never-ending supply of fertilizer.

t r o u b l e s h o o t i n g

When buying red worms, keep in mind that they come by the half pound, which goes a long way. Perhaps you can release some of them into a compost pile in your yard (but only if it's warm outside). You might also share some with friends who want to build worm condos of their own. If all else fails, and there is no vacancy in your condo, you can feed them to fish or reptile pets.

If you're lucky, you may know of a gardener or teacher who already has worms of their own. If so, you might ask to borrow some (it's just like asking a neighbor for a cup of sugar). If you do decide to borrow, don't forget to write a thank you.

Earthworms live in soil, not in manure piles.

Sort worms and return to the condo.

the good, the bad, and the ugly

INTRODUCTION

They may be creepy and crawly, but they are also fascinating. Once you start studying insects in their natural environment, you will develop respect and admiration for them. Insects all have certain common characteristics. They all have six legs and three separate body sections—the head, the thorax, and the abdomen. However, despite their common qualities, insects come in all different shapes, sizes, and colors; that's what makes them so interesting. Let the critter hunt begin!

materials

- **Glass collecting jars**
- **Magnifying glass**
- **Field guide to insects**
- **Butterfly net (optional)**
- **Black light (optional)**
- **White sheet**
- **Journal and pencil**

Look everywhere in the garden.

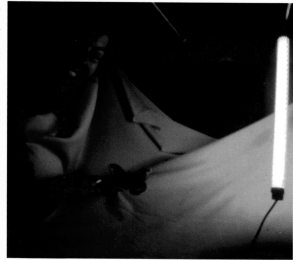

Use a black light to look at night.

PHOTO BY DAN GILREIN

what to do

1. Go outside and start looking around for insects. Look under rocks, in rotten fruit, in the soil—anywhere you can think of.

2. Put each specimen into a collecting jar along with a little reminder of home. In other words, if you find an insect on a particular type of leaf, put some of those same leaves into the collecting jar, so your specimen can enjoy its stay.

Look for spiders in the morning.

PHOTO BY DAN GILREIN

3. Examine the captured insects under a magnifying glass to fully appreciate their beauty. In your journal, record your observations and make a sketch of each specimen.

4. An up-close inspection will also help you make an identification. Look through a field guide to insects to determine what type of critters you have captured. Record their names in your journal. If you don't know, just write down the name of a similar-looking insect followed by a question mark.

5. If you have access to a black light, hang it outside on a summer night next to a white sheet. The ultraviolet light bounces off the sheet. This beautiful and strange light will attract night-flying insects from hundreds of yards away. Who knows what magnificent specimens you might find!

6. Release your specimens back into the approximate area of collection when you are done making your journal notes.

7. Repeat this process several times throughout the spring, summer, and fall.

- Did you find the same kinds of insects each time you did a collection?
- Did you see any damage to plants in your yard or garden that may have been caused by the types of insects you collected?
- How were you attracted to the insects you found? (Or in the case of moths, how were they attracted to you?) Did they make certain noises, have certain colors, and so forth? Or did you find them just by digging around?

explanation

Insects are numerous and easy to spot during the warm season. Insects are around in the winter too, but most are hard to find because they are "wintering" the cold weather in various shapes and forms (for protection) that you may not be familiar with. Adult insects are in full swing by the frost-free date and remain active until early fall.

Praying mantis.

PHOTO BY DAN GILREIN

Spotted golden slug.

PHOTO BY DAN GILREIN

conclusion

The more you handle insects, the more you grow to like them. Each living thing is good in its own way. We tend to label insects good, bad, or ugly based on how they affect us personally. A good insect would be one that eats other, harmful insects. We call an insect bad if it eats the vegetables, fruit, or flowers we had planned to eat or enjoy ourselves. And ugly is just a matter of taste. Beauty, as we all know, is in the eye of the beholder.

Aphids can weaken plants by sucking out its juices.

PHOTO BY DAN GILREIN

Bibliography

Aliki. *Fossils Tell of Long Ago*. New York: Cromwell, 1972.

————. *Wild and Woolly Mammoths*. New York: HarperCollins, 1996.

Greenaway, Theresa. *Worms*. Austin, Tex.: Raintree Steck-Vaughn Publishers, 1999.

Hood, Susan. *First Field Guide to Wildflowers*. New York: Scholastic, 1998.

Neilsen, Nancy J. *Carnivorous Plants: A First Book*. New York: Franklin Watts, 1992.

Pascoe, Elaine. *Slime Molds and Fungi*. Woodbridge, Conn.: Blackbirch Press, 1999.

Peterson, Roger Troy, and Margaret McKenny. *A Field Guide to Wildflowers*. Boston, Mass.: Houghton Mifflin, 1968.

Wilsdon, Christina. *First Field Guide to Insects*. New York: Scholastic, 1998.

Winckler, Suzanne, and May M. Rodgers. *Our Endangered Planet: Soil*. Minneapolis, Minn.: Lerner Publications, 1994.

Zim, Herbert. *Botany*. Racine, Wis.: Golden Press, 1970.

————. *Insects: A Guide to Familiar American Insects*. Racine, Wis.: Golden Press, 1951.

————. *Non-Flowering Plants*. Racine, Wis.: Golden Press, 1967.

RELATED READING

Here are some other fun Fulcrum books that will get you excited about garden experiments and explorations:

Cranshaw, Whitney, and Boris Kondratieff. *Bagging Big Bugs*. Golden, Colo.: Fulcrum, 1995.

Fredericks, Anthony D. *From Butterflies to Thunderbolts*. Golden, Colo.: Fulcrum, 1997.

Hardesty, Constance. *Grow Your Own Pizza*. Illustrated by Jeff McClung. Golden, Colo.: Fulcrum, 2000.

Kneidel, Sally. *Creepy Crawlies and the Scientific Method*. Golden, Colo.: Fulcrum, 1993.

————. *Slugs, Bugs and Salamanders*. Golden, Colo.: Fulcrum, 1997.

Krudwig, Vickie Leigh. *Cucumber Soup*. Illustrated by Craig McFarland Brown. Golden, Colo.: Fulcrum, 1999.

Wangberg, James K. *Do Bees Sneeze?* Golden, Colo.: Fulcrum, 1997.

Look for the monarch caterpillar.

PHOTO BY DAN GILREIN

Glossary

abdomen. The posterior (end) section of an insect's body.

absorb. To soak up.

adapt. To adjust to a particular situation.

air circulation. The movement or passage of air.

alga. A primitive organism that lacks a stem, roots, and leaves but whose cells do contain chlorophyll. (Plural: algae.)

artifact. A tool or ornament of historical interest.

backfill. To refill a hole with soil.

beneficial. Bringing a favorable result.

biological. Relating to a living organism.

blot. To soak up using an absorbent material.

botanist. A person who specializes in the study of plants.

buoyancy. The tendency to float.

carnivorous. Flesh-eating.

castings. Worm excrement (poop). Good food for plants.

chlorophyll. The green-colored matter in leaves that is an important part of photosynthesis.

chrysalis. The hard-shelled pupa of a butterfly.

circadian movements. Daily, predictable movements that occur over a 24-hour cycle.

commercial potting soil. Humanmade soil that can be bought and used readily.

compound leaf. A whole leaf that is composed of several similar leaflets.

conclusion. A determination based on the result or outcome of an experiment.

condominium. An apartment building that is owned rather than rented.

contrast. The prominence of one thing when compared to another.

culture. To grow microorganisms on a nutrient medium.

The monarch chrysalis.

PHOTO BY DAN GILREIN

Finally, the monarch butterfly.

PHOTO BY DAN GILREIN

cylinder. A shape like a tube.

decomposition. The process of organic material breaking down into basic elements.

dirt. Soil, earth.

diversity. A great variety.

document. To record an observation.

elastic. Stretchable.

endangered. Faced with the danger of extinction.

endosperm. A special structure within a seed that provides a germinating plant with food until the plant can obtain food on its own.

enzyme. A protein produced by the cells of a living organism to help the cells perform some function.

era. A period of time marked by a particular set of circumstances.

fallen tree. A dead tree that is lying on the ground.

flop. An experiment that has disappointing results.

fossils. Remains or traces of a living thing that have been embedded and preserved in the earth.

frond. The leaf of a fern.

frost-free date. The general date in specific areas where the night temperatures do not dip down below 33°F. Contact your local library or Cooperative Extension office to find out the date for each area.

Don't forget to add new pressed flowers to your collection each year.

fungus. A primitive plant that lacks chlorophyll, such as a yeast, mold, or mushroom.

germinate. To sprout or begin to grow.

gills. Thin structures underneath the cap of a mushroom where spores are made.

gland. A structure within a plant or animal that squirts out a special liquid.

harvest. To gather for a specific use.

herbarium. A collection of dried plants mounted and labeled for scientific study.

herd. To gather into a single group.

host plant. A special plant that provides food for larval (baby) insects.

humidity. The presence of moisture in the air.

hyphae. Threadlike branches of a fungus.

imprint. An impression made on the surface of something using pressure.

instinctively. In a manner that comes naturally.

iridescent. Producing a display of rainbowlike colors.

Jiffy Pot. Seedling pot made up of compressed peat moss pellets that swell up when soaked in water.

larvae. Insects in the earliest stage of metamorphosis.

leaf mold. Loose, rich soil made from decayed leaves.

leaflet. One of the separate blades or divisions of a compound leaf.

lure. To attract with the promise of reward.

Malva. A genus of plants that the larvae of painted ladies feed on.

media. Plural of medium (see below).

medium. A place where living things grow and thrive.

metamorphosis. The changing, for example, of a caterpillar into a butterfly.

microbe. A very tiny living thing. (Another word for microorganism.)

microorganism. A plant or animal so small that it cannot be seen without the aid of a microscope.

mimic. To copy or act like.

mineral. A naturally occurring soil substance needed by plants.

mold. A growth of very small fungi forming on animal or plant matter.

mulch. A protective layer placed above the soil to keep down weeds and to conserve soil moisture.

mount. To set in position.

mycelium. The body of a fungus, made up of hyphae.

nectar. A sweet liquid secreted by flowers to attract insects.

nitrogen. A nutrient needed for successful plant growth; gives plants their dark green color and aids in the growth of stems and leaves.

numerous. Many.

nylon. A synthetic yarn that is both strong and elastic.

Oasis. Floral product that secures cut flowers inside a cup.

optical illusion. A trick played on your eyes.

organism. A living thing.

paleontology. The study of fossils.

petiole. The stalk that attaches a leaf to the stem.

pH. A measure used to see how acidic or alkaline something is.

phenomenon. An unusual occurrence.

phosphorus. A necessary element for plant life.

Dill is a great plant for feeding caterpillars.

photosynthesis. A biological process where plant food is created from carbon dioxide, water, and salts in the presence of sunlight.

pinnule. One of the leaflets that make up a larger, compound leaf.

Plexiglas. A brand-name, clear plastic material that will not break under normal conditions.

pollinate. To move pollen from one flower to another flower for the purpose of fertilization.

potash. A type of fertilizer that contains potassium, an element needed for plant life.

preferable. Recommended.

primitive. Very old or very simple.

pupa. The transformation phase of an insect in which it is not able to move. (Plural: pupae.)

recovery. The process of returning to a normal condition.

rectangle. A shape like a box.

rhizoid. Rootlike structure of a fungus that acts like an anchor.

saturated. Soaked, filled, or loaded to the fullest extent possible.

sift. To examine closely and carefully.

sow. To scatter seed for growing.

specimen. A sample taken as a representative.

sporangiophore. In a fungus, a special branch of hyphae that holds a spore-making structure.

spore. The reproductive organ from a nonflowering plant such as a fern, moss, fungus, or lichen.

squeamish. Uneasy or uncomfortable.

stereo binocularscope. A special microscope that has two eyepieces for easier viewing of organisms that are too small to be seen with the naked eye.

submerged. Growing or remaining underwater.

Who says tests can't be fun?

symbiotic. Living together in a relationship of close association with some other living thing, often to the benefit of both organisms.

synthetic. Humanmade.

tendril. A climbing plant's threadlike leafless organ that is used to attach to things.

tepid. Moderately warm.

thorax. The portion of an insect's body between the head and the abdomen.

thrive. To grow vigorously.

tissue. A group of cells that perform a similar function.

translocation. The movement of something from one place to another.

trigger hair. A special structure of a plant that senses movement and causes a quick response.

xylem. Special structures in a plant that act like drinking straws and also help support the plant.

Index

PHOTO BY
DAN GILREIN